LOVE OF IRELAND

Love of Ireland

poems from the Irish

BRENDAN KENNELLY

89/, 621

THE MERCIER PRESS
CORK and DUBLIN

The Mercier Press Limited
4 Bridge Street Cork
24 Lower Abbey Street, Dublin 1

British Library Cataloguing in Publication Data
Love of Ireland.
  I. Kennelly, Brendan, 1936–
  891.6'21'008

ISBN 0 85342 888 3 paperback
ISBN 0 85342 901 4 hardback

Printed by The Leinster Leader Ltd., Naas, Co. Kildare.

ACKNOWLEDGEMENT

Some of these poems originally appeared in *A Drinking Cup* (Allen Figgis, 1970), *Selected Poems* (Kerrymount Press, 1985), and *Mary* (Aisling, 1987) and the author and publisher are grateful for permission to quote them in *Love of Ireland*. The illustrations in *Love of Ireland* are from *A Handbook of Celtic Ornament* by J. G. Merne and *Irish Carved Ornament* by H. S. Crawford and both books are published by The Mercier Press.

FOR DERMOT AND NOREEN EGAN

Contents

Love of Ireland

I send my blessing to Ireland,
    My mother.
It does my heart good
    To think of her.

I'm writing from Scotland, a good place
    For a man
To send a blessing to the land that knows
    All about rain.

I bless Patrick's city, Armagh
    Of the smooth soft-sodded wall.
I bless Derry of the streams
    Where learning is plentiful.

I send a blessing or two as well
    To Donegal.
My people found sanctuary there
    And decent burial.

I bless Assaroe of the oars, The Garravogue,
    The ancient Moy
And the tuneful haven of the river Bonnet
    Surpassing every estuary.

I make a litany of Lochs –
    Loch Erne, Loch Gill,
Loch Foyle of the wine,
    Clear, wooded, cool.

Next, the men of Ireland. First,
    My full and open
Blessing to all the men of Ulster.
    To all, that is, but one.

Then, the red-speared princes of Connaught,
    Every man and woman
And youth, ready warriors
    Of deep discipline.

I bless the people of Munster.
    Every man is my friend.
It's a shame beyond words that their rule
    Has come to an end.

Despite the dark foreigners settled in Meath
    I don't forget that place.
Its peaceful fountains, its miraculous land
    I bless.

I've never been to Leinster,
    Never seen its men
But I've heard enough of their bounty
    To bless them, one by one.

With my best will now I send
    A blessing to that grand
Company of modest hearts,
    The women of Ireland.

And all who beguile these women,
    I bless them too.
Modesty attracts magic. Put them together,
    What will they not do?

If the priests are kind, I bless
    Them as well.
If not, let them find their own
    Road to hell.

Blessing without equal I give
    To the makers of music.
There is no better way to praise
A poet's gift.

I bless the grass of Ireland,
    Her glens, woods,
Small hills with choice fruits
    On all sides.

I don't like leaving her.
    Why should I,
Knowing the voices of her rivers,
    The moods of her sky?

Yet in truth I have left her
    And can do nothing
But send across the sea today
    My heart's blessing.

My heart's blessing is not enough
    For that varied land
In whose praise a poet is glad to waste
    His right hand.

The Old Woman of Beare

The sea crawls from the shore
Leaving there
The despicable weed,
A corpse's hair.
In me,
The desolate withdrawing sea.

The Old Woman of Beare am I
Who once was beautiful.
Now all I know is how to die.
I'll do it well.

Look at my skin
Stretched tight on the bone.
Where kings have pressed their lips,
The pain, the pain.

I don't hate the men
Who swore the truth was in their lies.
One thing alone I hate —
Women's eyes.

The young sun
Gives its youth to everyone,
Touching everything with gold.
In me, the cold.

The cold. Yet still a seed
Burns there.
Women love only money now

But when
I loved, I loved
Young men.

Young men whose horses galloped
On many an open plain
Beating lightning from the ground,
I loved such men.

And still the sea
Rears and plunges into me,
Shoving, rolling through my head
Images of the drifting dead.

A soldier cries
Pitifully about his plight;
A king fades
Into the shivering night.

Does not every season prove
That the acorn hits the ground?
Have I not known enough of love
To know it's lost as soon as found?

I drank my fill of wine with kings,
Their eyes fixed on my hair;
Now among the stinking hags
I chew the cud of prayer.

Time was the sea
Brought kings as slaves to me;
Now I near the face of God
And the crab crawls through my blood.

I loved the wine
That thrilled me to my fingertips;
Now the mean wind
Stitches salt into my lips.

The coward sea
Slouches away from me.
Fear brings back the tide
That made me stretch at the side
Of him who'd take me briefly for his bride.

The sea grows smaller, smaller now.
Farther, farther it goes
Leaving me here where the foam dries
On the deserted land,
Dry as my shrunken thighs,
As the tongue that presses my lips,
As the veins that break through my hands.

My Story

Here's my story; the stag cries,
Winter snarls as summer dies.

The wind bullies the low sun
In poor light; the seas moan.

Shapeless bracken is turning red,
The wildgoose raises its desperate head.

Birds' wings freeze where fields are hoary.
The world is ice. That's my story.

Knockmealdown

In Knockmealdown the wolves
Howl in the echoing glens,
The wind cries,
The fierce deer bells near the chasm,
The crane screams over the crags,
The year dies.

The Storm

The devil's own night on the Great Moor
Where bucketing rain swells the flood;
The daft wind roars like a drunkard
Over the sheltering wood.

Flood

North-east the black shoals
Muscle the waters for food;
The sea, ever wanton and splendid,
Roars to a flood.

The Wind

The wind has broken us,
Crushed us,
Drowned us,
O King of the star-bright Kingdom,
Consumed us
As though we were timber
Caught in the crimson fires of heaven!

The Vikings

There's a wicked wind tonight,
Wild upheaval in the sea;
No fear now that the Viking hordes
Will terrify me.

The Wayside Fountain

At Cenn Esrach of the orchards
Bees seek every honeydrop;
In a sunlit thicket glitters
A drinking-cup.

Blackbird

Blackbird, you are happy
In the nest that shelters you,
O hermit without a bell
Your note is true.

The Blackbird's Song

The little bird is whistling now
From the tip of its yellow beak;
The blackbird on the yellow bough
Electrifies the lake.

Kate of Gornavilla

Have you been in Gornavilla
Have you seen in Gornavilla
The gay girl with golden hair
Sweet Kate of Gornavilla?

Whiter than the placid swan
Or the snow on the bending bough,
Her kiss as soft as the dew of dawn,
Dear Kate of Gornavilla.

Her song surpasses the young thrush
Or the blackbird in the whitethorn bush;
Like a ship in sail on a buoyant wave
Is Kate of Gornavilla.

She

She
White flower of the blackberry
Sweet flower of the raspberry
Pure herb of beauty
    Blesses the sight of my eyes.

She
Heart-pulse and blood-secret
Sweet flower of the apple
Hot sun in cold weather
    Between Christmas and Easter.

Happy the Man

Happy the man with a lover
In a long-prowed boat
High on the black wave
Leaving the dead land behind
As a risen man
Will quit the grave.

A Love-Song

Such a heart!
Should he leave, how I'd miss him.
Jewel, acorn, youth.
Kiss him!

The Son of the King of Moy

The son of the King of Moy
Found a girl in a green dell,
Of the rich abounding fruit
She gave him his fill.

Etain

Who will sleep with Etain tonight?
    That's still unknown.
One thing is certain though—
    Etain won't sleep alone.

How Glad are the Small Birds

How glad are the small birds
    That rise and sing on one bough;
How near to each other! How far
    Is my love from me now!

White as new milk, sweet as the fiddle,
    Bright as the summer sun
Is she. Dear God in heaven,
    Free me from pain!

Kisses

Keep your kiss, young girl,
    Away with you tonight,
In your kiss I find no taste
    Though your teeth are white.

I kissed a girl for love.
    Sweeter taste I'll never find
In any woman's kiss
    Till time is out of mind.

Until the graceful son of God
    Makes that girl pass my way,
I shall love none, old or young,
    Let her kiss taste how it may.

The Blackthorn Pin

Sweet red-lipped girl, for many years
    You have been loved by men.
Your cloak should bear a golden brooch
    And not a blackthorn pin.

O graceful girl, just to all,
    Whom none could ever   win
Why should your yellow cloak show but
    A blackthorn pin?

Wear it then! It is your secret
    And will not be told:
Give the blackthorn pin another hour;
    Then raise the gold.

The Indifferent Mistress

She is my love
Though she makes my life a hell,
Dearer, though she makes me sick,
Than one who would make me well.

She is my dear
Who has reduced me to a slave,
She'd never let one sigh for me
Or lay a stone on my grave.

She is my treasure
Whose eye is stern with pride,
She'd never put an arm under my head
Or lie at my side.

She is my secret
Who won't speak a word to me,
Who won't listen to anything under the sun
Or turn an eye on me.

My plight is sad.
To a lonely death I move.
She who spurns me, only she
Can be my love.

Hate Goes Just as Far as Love

Woman full of hate for me
    Do you not recall the night
When we together, side by side,
    Knew love's delight?

If you remembered woman, how,
    While the sun lost its heat,
You and I grew hot—
    But why repeat?

Do you recall my lips on yours,
    Soft words you said,
And how you laid your curving arm
    Under my head?

Or do you remember, O sweet shape,
    How you whispered passionately
That God Almighty had never made
    A man like me?

I gave all my heart to you,
    Gave all, yet could not give enough;
Now, I've your hate. O skin like flowers,
    This hate goes just as far as love.

If a man believes he loves a woman
    And that she loves him too,
Let him know one thing for certain—
    It is not true.

Reconciliation

Do not torment me, woman,
  Let our two minds be as one,
Be my mate in my own land
  Where we may live till life is done.

Put your mouth against my mouth
  You whose skin is fresh as foam,
Take me in your white embrace
  And let us love till kingdom come.

Slender graceful girl, admit
  Me soon into your bed,
Discord, pain will disappear
  When we stretch there side by side.

For your sweet sake, I will ignore
  Every girl who takes my eye,
If it's possible, I implore
  You do the same for me.

As I have given from my heart
  Passion for which alone I live,
Let me now receive from you
  The love you have to give.

The Holy Man

A trapped bird
A wrecked ship
An empty cup
A withered tree
Is he
Who scorns the will of the King above.

Pure gold
Bright sun
Filled wine-cup
Happy beautiful holy
Is he
Who does the will of the King of love.

Saint, Bird, Angel

Saint Anfaidh walked alone
    Where a thin stream was flowing
And there he saw a little bird
    Sorrowing.

'God,' he thought, 'What's happening?
    I cannot think;
But till I understand, I shall not
    Eat or drink.'

An angel stood beside him
    And quietly said,
'Mo Lua, gentle son of Ocha
    Has just died.

All living things lament him,
    He was loved by all,
He never killed a living thing
    Great or small.

The beast laments him with his cry,
    Man with a tender word,
And look, beside you, grieving stands
    A little bird.'

Jesus on the Sabbath

Jesus, son of the living God,
    Was five years old; one day
He blessed twelve small pools
    And fenced them in with clay.

Twelve little birds he shaped,
    Passeres they are called;
He made them on the Sabbath
    Of clay without a fault.

A certain Jew attacked him,
    Son of the living God,
And to his father Joseph
    He led him by the hand.

'Keep and eye on your son, Joseph,
    How badly he behaves!
Imagine! On the Sabbath
    He makes images of birds.'

Jesus clapped his hands,
    His young voice they heard
And then before their eyes
    He scattered the little birds.

He said, 'That you may know who made you
    Return to your homes tonight,'
Then someone shouted that he heard
    The cries of birds in flight.

Jesus at School

The wise Zacharias said,
    'This lad is wonderful
And he'd be a hundred times better
    If he went to school.'

Jesus went with Zacharias
    Who wished to teach him to read;
'Here's the alphabet, boy. Say *A*.'
    The all-knowing head

Refused. Zacharias used the stick.
    Jesus said then,
'Strike an anvil, what is the lesson?
    The anvil teaches the man.'

Quietly then the boy
    Proved that his words were true,
Speaking to old Zacharias
    More than Zacharias knew.

Said the wise Zacharias then,
    'Take this boy from me now,
I can't give any answer.
    Leave me with what I know.'

Rome

To go to Rome
Is great trouble, small profit.
The King you have in mind
(Unless you bring Him in your heart)
You'll never find.

God's Praises

Only a fool would fail
To praise God in His might
When the tiny mindless birds
Praise Him in their flight.

The Bell

I'd sooner keep my tryst
    With that sweet little bell
The night of a bad winter mist
    Than risk a ravenous female.

Christ's Bounty

I pray you, Christ, to change my heart,
    To make it whole;
Once you took on flesh like mine,
    Now take my soul.

Ignominy and pain you knew,
    The lash, the scourge,
You, the perfect molten metal
    Of my darkened forge.

You make the bright sun bless my head,
    Put ice beneath my feet,
Send salmon swarming in the tides,
    Give crops of wheat.

When Eve's wild children come to you
    With prayerful words,
You crowd the rivers with fine fish,
    The sky with birds.

You make the small flowers thrive
    In the wholesome air,
You spread sweetness through the world.
    What miracle can compare?

The Wild Man and the Church

On the clean watercress
I make a decent feast;
Why should I sit at table
With a bleating priest?

I love the voices
Of wolves in the dark glen;
Not for me the gentle talk
Of studious men.

With ceremony in their long halls
They drink and sing;
I cup cold water in my fist
From a pure spring.

God Bless Munster

May God bless Munster
Woman, man and boy,
May he lavish on that land
His infinite gift of joy.
May God bless Munster
Every plain and field,
May green grasses grow there
And great crops of wheat.
Bless every flagstone
Every mountainy ledge
Every glen and meadow
Valley, fort and ridge.
May Munster families grow
To equal the sands of the sea;
God's blessing on Munster
Through all eternity.

The Tree of Life

Round the Tree of Life the flowers
Are ranged, abundant, even;
Its crest on every side spreads out
On the fields and plains of Heaven.

Glorious flocks of singing birds
Celebrate their truth,
Green abounding branches bear
Choicest leaves and fruit.

The lucid flocks maintain their song
In the changeless weather,
A hundred feathers for every bird,
A hundred tunes for every feather.

On Mael Mhuru the Poet

Tara has not known
Ireland has not seen
Choice earth has not lain
On one
Like the gentle pure Mael Mhuru.

Life has never lost
There has not gone to dust
The earth has not possessed
A man
Like the gentle pure Mael Mhuru.

On the Death of William Gould

All over Ireland—why this chill?
   Why this foul mist?
Why the crying birds?
   Why do the heavens mutter
      Such wrathful words?

Why this blow to a poet?
   Why do the Feale and Shannon tremble?
Why does the wild sky spill
   Such venomous rain
      On plain and hill?

What has put song in chains
   And nobles in bonds?
Why do God's own bold
   Servants and prophets
      Walk shocked and appalled?

The cause of their grief
   Is that fair William Gould
Has died in France.
   Christ! No wonder this pall
      Darkens the land.

Giver of horses and cloaks,
   Of silver and gold,
Silk, wine, meat, bread;
   This giver, this generous giver
      Is dead.

Hospitality in Ancient Ireland

God in Heaven!
The door of my house will always be
Open to every traveller.
May Christ open His to me!

If you have a guest
And deny him anything in the house,
It's not the guest you hurt.
It's Christ you refuse.

The Wild Man of the Woods

What a dismal life!
    Never to lie in a warm bed;
In this cold frosty place
    The wind hammers my head.

Flakes of ice on the wind,
    A feeble sun—no more
But the skeleton tree
    Defining the moor.

My back to the black rain,
    Stepping where deer have passed,
I face the road again
    This morning of bitter frost!

The Cliff of Alteran

As Sweeny ranged over Connaught
    He came to a lonely glen
Where a stream poured over a cliff
    And many holy men

Togethered. Trees, heavy with fruit,
    Grew there by the score.
There were sheltering ivy bowers
    And apple trees galore.

Deer, hares and swine were there.
    By the warm cliffs fat seals slept.
Sweeny watched while through his heart
    The raving madness swept.

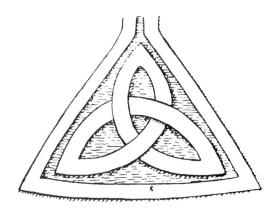

O'Neill's Letter to Sir John McCoughleyn

My greetings to you, McCoughleyn,
    I got your letter,
Sweet words and nonsense.
    I thought you'd do better.

As far as I'm concerned
    Whoever won't fight with me
And be ready to give his life—
    He's my enemy.

Therefore, whatever you do,
    Just let me say how I feel—
Hurt me, by God I'll hurt you
    As much as I can. O'Neill.

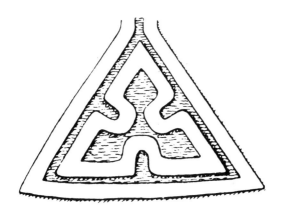

On the Murder of David Gleeson, Bailiff

Let the poets laugh and rejoice,
    Let the robber death be forgiven
        And no words of pity be said;
Cry it aloud to high heaven—
    The Bailiff Gleeson is dead.

Ireland is happier now,
    That skinflint is gone to the devil,
        To the fate that he merited well,
Condemned to foul quarters of evil
    And the torments of hell.

Ugly venomous scum,
    His trade was cursed in the village,
        He was glad to see others fail,
To see good folk pitched into prison.
    May he rot in Lucifer's jail!

Brazen, spiteful and crooked,
    His trade drew the poet's fury,
        May the hand that ended his life
Be rewarded for doing its duty.
    May his spirit dwell ever in strife!

It is pleasant to hear in Cork
    Of Gleeson's yellow carcass,
        How he died without a friend,
Hanging on high from the gallows.
    May his suffering never end!

Fionn's Generosity

Turn brown leaves to gold
On an autumn day,
Turn white waves to silver—
Fionn would give all away.

Boor

A horse for a song of praise
He should give
But he doesn't know how.
He gives what his nature permits—
A cow.

Valentine Brown

Because all night my mind inclines to wander and
   to rave,
Because the English dogs have made Ireland a green
   grave,
Because all of Munster's glory is daily trampled down,
I have travelled far to meet you, Valentine Brown.

Because the might of Cashel is withered all away,
And the badger skulks in Brian's house, seeking out
   his prey,
And the laughing kings are all deprived of sceptre and
   of crown,
I have travelled far to meet you, Valentine Brown.

Because the deer in Ross's Wood run no longer free,
And the crows of death are croaking now on top of
   every tree,
And never a fish is seen to leap where mountain
   streams come down,
I have travelled far to meet you, Valentine Brown.

Dernish ravaged in the west, her good lord gone as
   well,
Some foreign city has become our refuge and our hell.
Wounds that hurt a poet's soul can rob him of renown:
I have travelled far to meet you, Valentine Brown.

Uncertainty

Each night, morning, on land, sea,
I realise again and again
I must die. But why? Or how?
Or when?

Hope

Time has triumphed, the wind has scattered all,
Alexander, Caesar, empires, cities are lost,
Tara and Troy flourished a while and fell
And even England itself, maybe, will bite the dust.

County Mayo

Now with the Springtime there's a great stretch in
     the days
And after Brigid's feastday I'll gather my traps and go,
Since I took it into my head, no chance that I'll delay
Till I find myself in the middle of the county Mayo.

In the town of Claremorris I'll spend the first gay
     night
And in Balla behind it I'll drink porter galore,
Then I'll hit for Kiltimagh and a full month's delight,
A bare two miles away from Ballinamore.

My heart swells and lifts just like a rising tide,
Sprightly as a lively wind that scatters the mist and
     snow,
When I think of Carra and Gallen side by side,
Scahaveela's welcome and the great plains of Mayo.

At last to Killaden, God's own garden you might say,
The finest fruit in Ireland, the pride of Mayomen,
If I were standing now among my people there,
The curse of age would wither, I'd be a boy again.

Her Head

My eyes once more adore at night
My girl's shapely head
But see, in cruel morning light
Worms bite into the dead.

Have I really known in deepest sleep
The joy her sweet voice gave?
Or is it truth that cuts to the quick?
My heart is sick by the sullen grave.

The Dead Wife

My soul left me last night
    Gone to God
My wife's body
    Wrapped in a linen shroud.

From this weak stalk, a white
    Blossom has been plucked.
My life's fruitful branch, my own
    Heart's darling has been ripped

From me. I am alone tonight, O God,
    In this crooked world of your making.
Light was the weight of the body
    That was here last night, O King.

It breaks my heart
    To look at that bed.
The woman who stretched there
    Is dead.

A gentle rhythm in her face,
    She lay at my side a long while.
Her voice was the shadow
    Of the hazel.

She was there, in that bed, alive,
    Beside me.
My heart is the woman
    Who has left me.

My body has passed out of my control.
    It is hers alone.
I am a body in two pieces
    Since the gentle one is gone.

She was one of my feet, one of my sides,
    I belonged in her body,
She was one of my hands,
    One of my eyes,

She was half of my body,
    The very half of my soul.
How I have been cut in two
    Is not easy to tell.

My first love was for her eyes,
    Her breasts, hands, feet.
Her body belonged to no man before me.
    I know that.

Twenty years we spent together
    Our days sweeter by the year.
She had eleven children.
    I loved her thin fingers.

Though I am alive I am dead
    Since my hazelnut fell
And twisting heaven turned this world
    Into clear hell.

Let no man check me now.
    Weeping is not forbidden.
Ruin is the only guest in my house
    O my glowing woman.

The King of Hosts, the King of Roads
 Swept her in His displeasure.
No blame to her that she
 Left me here.

O King of bells and churchyards
 I see her hand, I am tortured
Because her hand that never swore false oath
 Is not under my head.

Thoughts Astray

Shame to all my thoughts now
    How they skip and stray,
This will be my danger
    On the Judgment day.

At the singing of the psalms
    My thoughts sing another road,
Giddy, jumpy, always
    Forgetting about God.

With wanton women
    Beckoning in the mind
Through woods, through cities – swifter
    Than any wind

Now in a sweet meadow
    Now in a place of shame
Now in a banquet-hall
    In a country without a name.

Unhelped by even the slightest craft
    They make light of every sea;
One leap from earth to heaven
    Proves their agility

And if I doubted that, they
    Somersault again,
Forsaking careful angels
    For truant men.

They run the race of folly
    Far and near;
After a daft spin through time and space
    They swagger back here

And if I shackled their hands, fettered their feet,
    Tethered them to my own breast,
Do you think that would stop them?
    They'd never rest.

Sword and whip are helpless
    To keep them down,
Eels bellying through grasses
    Of the mind's moist ground.

No lock of jail or dungeon
    Can hold them back,
No man-made chains will keep them
    From their crazy track.

O Christ
    To you such things are clear,
Help me to net these thoughts
    To still them here

Locked in my mind's cold cell,
    Feeling the chill
Discipline that makes me hope
    I do your will.

The Harrowing of Hell

I speak of God's resurrection in Asia.
    I boast of a triumphant visit.
No beauty that I have seen or could conjure
    Can equal it.

Men crucify the guiltless Christ
    As you have heard.
To the malefactor it is an unjust wound,
    A spike in the righteous blood.

A grave was dug for Jesus Christ
    After His crucifixion.
A guard of men protected the grave
    Which our Creator had won.

He rose on the third day, bringing
    Dismay on those who'd killed
Him. His face became threatening.
    He turned His face to Hell.

The lord of that house said, 'There comes towards you
    A small deceiver.
As His body was shattered, let not
    His soul go unriven.

Prepare your bellows, pick up your sledge-hammers,
    There's no time to waste.
Let not the breaking of this deceiver be
    A second time an idle boast.

It was I who tempted Eve, out of her
    White-tipped hands, out of her trusting bones,
Out of her eyes so soft and grey
    Under the appletree of transgression.

I slid into the form of a serpent,
    I beguilded that woman after we had
Slipped together, all was quiet,
    Under cover of the wood.

I said to her — my words false
    And beautiful —
"Take this apple, Eve, it is the sweetest,
    It has the fragrance of Adam's isle."

Eve takes the apple. She gives half
    To her mate, as she must.
Their children and their race fall in him.
    This is not unjust.

I deceive Eve and Adam as bitterly,
    As ungently as I can.
I inject into the air of heaven
    My singular poison.

It was I who found, though manly his torment,
    For the seed of Eve
And Adam, to check their welfare, a man
    To spy on the deceiver.

I gave, at the right moment to faltering Judas
    My unfaltering word.
I grew rich in the moment he betrayed
    His Lord.

I beat a spike into the feet
    Nails into the palms
I left him in a mean black place
    Earth pressing above him.'

We were only a short while in this converse
    Which I am relating to you when,
A marvel to the swarthy host, hell
    Became a fair plain.

'What,' said Adam's children, 'Is
    This light within
Which, long as we are here, we
    Have never seen?'

'Can God's only son be at the door,'
    Said Adam, thrilled,
'To bring forth His race as it has been
    Foretold?'

'One day,' continued Adam, 'I sent my son
    To Paradise
Of the bright-stemmed appletrees.
    Before his eyes

By the withered tree where I and my
    Great seed
Fell, he saw a child,
    Comely, soft-eyed.

The child covered the bare tree with branches
    Green and leafy and lush.
His fingers were shaking the appletree
    Till it grew fresh.

I stayed waiting on the plain
    For my son Seth.
He came talking of the tree and the child.
    His words were sweet.

That young child,' said Adam, 'Is He
    Who is approaching now.
It will take the bad pain away from men —
    The child's way with the bare tree'.

We had not long to wait till Christ's hand
    Knocked at the door.
There was reason in this plot until the King
    Asked if He might enter.

The prisoners within were glad
    To hear a friend's voice.
Their yeomen were not sad,
    Their elders were merry.

David, Abraham, Isaac, Moses
    And children thought
A madman was blasting the kocker.
    'Who makes this noise without?'

Queried the people of Hell. 'Whose hand,'
    Asked each trapped man,
'Has struck the knocker
    Like a stone?'

'I am Christ. I am standing here at the door.
    I am the friend of man.
I am the Son of Mary,
    The Virgin.'

They all cower back for fear
    Of Jesus the curly-haired.
The door breaks in on top of them.
    Every churl is a coward.

The Lord sprang in, Mary's only Son,
    Creative God.
There was no sound but ah! and ah!
    He said,

'Rise up and stand!' His voice at one
    With His eyes.
'Anna's work is showing in you now.
    Children of Adam, arise!'

'Give me your hand, Adam,' He said.
    Adam stretched forth the hand
That had been wounded by the apple.
    Now there was no wound.

Eve followed Adam. Then, like a chain out of hell,
    All the others followed her.
This was no place for a heedless person.
    This was no time to falter.

His people came forth with him then
    Every man a flower
Adam's seed in every field
    At the heels of their ancestor.

Certain distinguished men of learning
    Have, it is rumoured, thought
That Jesus brought out of Hell only those
    Who deserved to be brought.

Others, who lack perfect faith, say there is no man
    White or black, whom He will
Not bring forth, one and all, in the goodness of time,
    Out of Hell.

He gave Adam and his company
    Into Michael's charge, outside.
Then He Himself went after them,
    Taking the Creator's road.

May the Creator to Whom they travelled
    And that Son whom we live to praise
Place the taste of victory on our lips
    Over the grave.

A Cry for Art O'Leary

My love
The first time I saw you
From the top of the market
My eyes covered you
My heart went out to you
I left my friends for you
Threw away my home for you

What else could I do?

You got the best rooms for me
All in order for me
Ovens burning for me
Fresh trout caught for me
Choice meat for me

In the best of beds I stretched
Till milking-time hummed for me

You made the whole world
Pleasing to me

White rider of love!

I love your silver-hilted sword
How your beaver hat became you
With its band of gold
Your friendly homespun suit
Revealed your body
Your pin of glinting silver
Glittered in your shirt

On your horse in style
You were sensitive pale-faced
Having journeyed overseas
The English respected you
Bowing to the ground
Not because they loved you
But true to their hearts' hate

They're the ones who killed you
Darling of my heart

My lover
My love's creature
Pride of Immokelly
To me you were not dead
Till your great mare came to me
Her bridle dragging ground
Her head with your startling blood
Your blood upon the saddle
You rode in your prime
I didn't wait to clean it
I leaped across my bed
I leaped then to the gate
I leaped upon your mare
I clapped my hands in frenzy
I followed every sign
With all the skill I knew
Until I found you lying
Dead near a furze bush
Without pope or bishop
Or cleric or priest
To say a prayer for you

Only a crooked wasted hag

Throwing her cloak across you

I could do nothing then
In the sight of God
But go on my knees
And kiss your face
And drink your free blood

My man!
Going out the gate
You turned back again
Kissed the two children
Threw a kiss at me
Saying, 'Eileen, woman, try
To get this house in order,
Do your best for us
I must be going now
I'll not be home again.'
I thought that you were joking
You my laughing man

My man!
My Art O'Leary
Up on your horse now
Ride out to Macroom
And then to Inchigeela
Take a bottle of wine
Like your people before you
Rise up
My Art O'Leary
Of the sword of love

Put on your clothes
Your black beaver

Your black gloves
Take down your whip
Your mare is waiting
Go east by the thin road
Every bush will salute you
Every stream will speak to you
Men and women acknowledge you

They know a great man
When they set eyes on him

God's curse on you, Morris
God's curse on your treachery
You swept my man from me
The man of my children
Two children play in the house
A third lives in me

He won't come alive from me

My heart's wound
Why was I not with you
When you were shot
That I might take the bullet
In my own body?
Then you'd have gone free
Rider of the grey eye
And followed them
Who'd murdered me

My man!
I look at you now
All I know of a hero
True man with true heart

Stuck in a coffin
You fished the clean streams
Drank nightlong in halls
Among frank-breasted women

I miss you

My man!
I am crying for you
In far Derrynane
In yellow-appled Carren
Where many a horseman
And vigilant woman
Would be quick to join
In crying for you
Art O'Leary
My laughing man

O crying women
Long live your crying
Till Art O'Leary
Goes back to school
On a fateful day
Not for books and music

But for stones and clay

My man!
The corn is stacked
The cows are milking
My heart is a lump of grief
I will never be healed
Till Art O'Leary
Comes back to me

I am a locked trunk
The key is lost
I must wait till rust
Devours the screw

O my best friend
Art O'Leary
Son of Conor
Son of Cadach
Son of Lewis
East from wooded glens
West from girlish hills
Where rowan-berries grow
Yellow nuts budge from branches
Apples laugh like small suns
As once they laughed
Throughout my girlhood
It is no cause for wonder
If bonfires lit O'Leary country
Close to Ballingeary
Or holy Gougane Barra
After the clean-gripping rider
The robust hunter
Panting towards the kill
Your own hounds lagged behind you
O horseman of the summoning eyes
What happened you last night?
My only whole belief
Was that you could not die
For I was your protection

My heart! My grief!

My man! My darling!

In Cork
I had this vision
Lying in my bed:
A glen of withered trees
A home heart-broken
Strangled hunting-hounds
Choked birds
And you
Dying on a hillside
Art O'Leary
My one man
Your blood running crazily
Over earth and stone

Jesus Christ knows well
I'll wear no cap
No mourning dress
No solemn shoes
No bridle on my horse
No grief-signs in my house
But test instead
The wisdom of the law

I'll cross the sea
To speak to the King
If he ignores me
I'll come back home
To find the man
Who murdered my man

Morris, because of you
My man is dead

Is there a man in Ireland
To put a bullet through your head?

Women, white women of the mill
I give my love to you
For the poetry you made
For Art O'Leary
Rider of the brown mare
Deep women-rhythms of blood
The fiercest and the sweetest
Since time began
Singing of this cry I womanmake
For my man

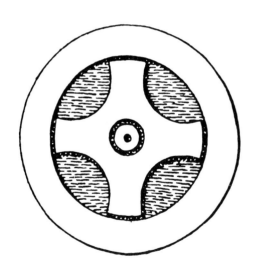

The Island Protected by a Bridge of Glass

They rowed to a fortified island
  A stronghold gripped the ground
A high fence made of brass
    Rose all around.

Around the fence was a pool
    High above moody seas
Before it (words are ashamed)
    This bridge of glass,

Máel Dúin's swift young men
    Climbed up but fell away
Like stray seed to the earth—
    A tax they had to pay.

A woman approached
    Her face was innocent
Folly had not touched her
    Her body was radiant.

A hem of red gold adorned
    Her cloak
They saw silver sandals on her feet
    When she came close.

A brooch of silver on her cloak
    She wore
A master's hand had inset
    Woven gold.

Gold was the yellow hair
	Of her head
Grace was her companion
	When she moved.

In the lower part of the bridge of glass
	Like a sanctuary, a well
Protected by a bulky lid, lay
	Deep and full.

The woman poured her liquor
	Not for the men
Who stood there in her presence.
	She ignored them.

Germán spoke out at last
	Loud-voiced, brazen-nerved;
'You pour the best drink in the world
	But we are not served.'

She closed the fort and left them.
	Music rose
Like waves of power chanting how
	Beautiful she was.

Her choir lulled them to sleep
	As had been enjoined.
Next day she came among them
	Unashamed.

They were like that for three days
	Her music played
No banqueting-hall could be seen
	No meat wine bread.

She led them to a huge house
  Sea-voices rose and fell
A feast for kings she gave them
  Drink for all.

The woman treated them
  Like men who'd won their fame.
She did them the honour of calling
  Each man by his name.

When she was asked to satisfy
  The leader's lust for her
She said that she knew nothing
  Of his desire.

'You've lost the words that made me
  Open to you.
Ask the secret of the island, the bridge of glass,
  And you shall know'.

They woke to light in their own boat
  Morning had come
The sea extended like a man's ignorance
  The island was gone.

Saint Brigid's Prayer

I'd like to give a lake of beer to God.
   I'd love the Heavenly
Host to be tippling there
      For all eternity.

I'd love the men of Heaven to live with me,
      To dance and sing.
If they wanted, I'd put at their disposal
      Vats of suffering.

White cups of love I'd give them
      With a heart and a half;
Sweet pitchers of mercy I'd offer
      To every man.

I'd make Heaven a cheerful spot
      Because the happy heart is true.
I'd make the men contented for their own sake.
      I'd like Jesus to love me too.

I'd like the people of Heaven to gather
      From all the parishes around.
I'd give a special welcome to the women,
      The three Marys of great renown.

I'd sit with the men, the women and God
      There by the lake of beer.
We'd be drinking good health forever
      And every drop would be a prayer.

Mary

Mary, listen to me, I am praying
   To you with every sense.
Turn to me now, Mother of the King
   Of the elements.

I remember your own mother's story
   I've heard it here and there
She was a gentle girl with dark brows
   And heavy wavy hair.

That is Anna, grandmother of God,
   Wonders rippling in her name,
Most dignified of women, married three
   Husbands in her time.

She had a daughter by each man,
   Three beautiful children,
Their bodies smooth, their hair wavy
   And heavy in wind and sun.

I see their blue eyes seeing me
   In their heart-lifting company.
Everyone alive loves to be with the three
   Women called Mary.

The three Marys took three husbands,
   Three women with luxuriant
Heavy wavy hair became slow-footed
   And pregnant.

The three women had three sons,
    Three lights cutting through cloud
To illuminate dark hearts, dark places.
    The youngest of these was God.

One of the women was the mother of James,
    From the worst troubles she went free.
One was Mary the mother of John, their names
    Have not appeared in poetry.

You are Mary the Mother of God
    Nobody touches your fame;
The king of heaven, branch split in three,
    Was in your womb;
Your womb, though He rules undreamable fields, is
    His true kingdom.

Let me enter your house, your stronghold,
    My dear one, great Mary,
O yellow gold, o flourishing
    Apple tree,

O my food, clothes on my body,
    Mother, kinswoman,
Love of my dark heart, protect
    Your kinsman.

Because your Son is my kinsman
    It is right
You should protect me, man alone,
    By day and night
There where you are, here where I am
    At your gate.

Until your Husband did my work, Mary,
    My heart was a field of black flowers.
It is time for me to pluck them now
    And scatter them to the four quarters
Watching the driven petals become stars,
    The stars become feathers.

O Mother of God, whose hair is bright and deep,
    Let us make peace to-day
Like my fingers would make silk play
    About your body.
Do not be angry, Mary, o red gold
    In a vessel of clay,
If a star knows what it means to shine
    I know what it means to pray.

Am I not kin with your Husband?
    Do we not share the same blood?
Am I not, like his hands, his thighs,
    Moulded by God?

Listen, Mary, listen to my poem,
    My poem is what it is,
I want no reward, I want to sing why
    Every glory but yours passes.

I want to sing my prayer: o black brow,
    Great tree, fertile garden,
Most beloved of women, I ask here and now
    For heaven,
The only gift worth asking for.
    Let it be given.

When I consider you, Mary, you have no equal
    Among living or dead;
All who have lived and will ever live
    Dream in a corner of your head.

Your Son, your Husband, your father,
    One, in you, one,
There, close, resting, peaceful, one, in you,
    God, man, man.

Your breast, your hair,
    Your son, your Husband,
Together, resting, one, there, there
    Where love is unconfined.

Taking refuge in valley after valley,
    Safe, unknown,
You found Him, He you, agile Boy,
    Slow-moving woman.

He pays attention to your hair, he is
    Your burden, your protection,
You must protect him, he is always in your care,
    You will not let him down.

You pay attention to him, your white
    Breast in his hand,
When you washed his body
    Love was unconfined.

There is something about you, Mary, something
    Nobody has every guessed
But the baby at his ease drinking
    Milk from your breast

Helping God grow into the dream
    Where a man is lost
Wandering like a feather in the wind,
    Tossed, again, tossed, forever, tossed.

I curse the man who insults you
    He's wrong from start to end
If you are not what I dream you are
    Best dreams are poisoned.

Thieves and murderers dock in my head now
    I must make way
I do not doubt you, murderers and thieves
    Have their own words to say.

God said Himself in you because
    He is His own wish,
He did not lie with you, your womb was full
    As the belly of a fish.

Without you, Mary, light, dark, work, thought, dream
    Are all confusion.
When I listen to your words I become
    A clear-headed man.

Your Son has your heavy hair
    Something of your eyes
Awake when the world sleeps, most tender
    And heart-breakingly wise.

Your face is angelbright, I hear
    The ages in one breath,
I see your slender hands, I owe you
    One poem, my heart's truth.

73

Your hair is yellow now, your eyes closed,
    When your hands work they adore
The work put into your hands
    By your Creator
Working to make you the woman who'll create
    Him in you for me forever.

No woman like you has lived
    No woman like you has died
You begin to be beyond the limits of dream
    Like your dreaming God
Trying to find you where you find Him
    Wandering in your blood
Like a feather tossed like a fierce wish
    For calm solitude.

Give me hospitality, give me drink,
    A real feast
While the words honey from your mouth
    And spill on your breasts.

Your Husband will not be jealous if I
    Pray to you like this.
This is my way. This is my poem.
    I love your white teeth.

I love the thought of your hair, the thought
    Of your hospitality.
Do not abandon me to any other judgment.
    What I offer, take. What I ask, give me.

Let us enjoy this feast, Mary, in the light
    And shade of your shapely form:
Accept this poem of my blood,
    God-creating woman.

If you want to take over my house,
    Do.
Where no poem reaches, there you live
    Beautiful and true.

I can live without others' hospitality,
    Without women, horses, hounds,
I can live without the dear attention
    Of my friends

If you lift the dark brow to me,
    The face like a calf's blood
So that I glimpse in the sea-deep hair
    The hiding-place of God.

Lift your feet to me, your hands
    Your eyes your hair
Let my dream mingle with yours
    Feasting together.

Who Will Buy A Poem?

Question! Who will buy a poem?
  It's genuine stuff,
Guaranteed to make you immortal
    Or fall in love.

Though I have a rich poem to offer
    I have walked all Munster,
Every market from cross to cross, and found
    Only a sneer.

A pound is little, but no man or woman
    Will go to that expense.
Neither the Irish nor the English will budge
    From their indifference.

Poetry is dirt on the road now.
    People don't care.
I should retire and make combs
    To help them scour their hair.

Poetry dies because decent people
    Vanish from the earth.
I received cattle and the price of cattle.
    I got what I was worth.

If generous men and women die out
    A poet loses his desire
To celebrate the noble hearts,
    To praise all that they are.

These praising ways must be encouraged
By the bountiful and strong
Or the crops will fail, the cattle die,
The children turn out wrong.

I'm a proud country turning to bad land.
I ask my idle question:
People of Ireland, who will buy a poem?
No-one. No-one.

Song Of Summer

Summer the king of seasons
Wears a cloak of all colours
Nothing can stop the blackbird singing
When he gets the hint of morning

The thieving cuckoo is glad
To call his welcome
I can't imagine bad weather
The land is home

Panic startles the deer's heart
The sea is easy
And seems to be asleep
Flowers are queenly

Hard-grafting bees
Rob the blossoms of honey
Cows browse on hillsides
Ants double their industry

The skilled fingers of a breeze
Play the harp of the forest
Close your eyes you hear music
North south east and west

The high cold waterfall
Longs for the warm pool
Drops into it as into a bed
This love knows itself well

Swallows link hill to hill
Their flight is worth long study
The stammering quagmire utters itself
Stubbornly

The bog comes into its own
Host to cuckoo and hare
If a boy is not strong now
He'll never be a warrior

Men flourish like wheat
Women are proud as fields
All things hope to be perfect
I begin to believe in peace

A flock of birds descends
Into a stretch of grass
There is a rustling a whispering
A sense of singing and laughter

I have this longing to race horses
All over the land from shore to shore
Come with me each will find
How wild is the other

But not just yet. Listen,
That great-hearted singer, the lark,
Is singing how we feel.
The joy of summer is God's work.

Uncertainty

You plant a tree.
  Will you be here to pluck
The apples? When the tree becomes itself
    Will you be here to look?

Think of not being.
    You excel at fixing
Props. But will
    You pluck an apple?

When it is ripe in your hand
    Will you eat it?
In this garden of shining sprays
    Death may visit.

It is not prudent to watch
    Appletrees growing
And in the abundant green orchard
    Not to think of nothing.

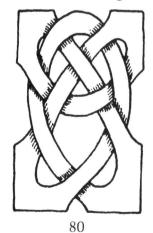

Withered Hands

I have loved, hunted, fought and killed
  Here and in other lands.
A life's pleasure is a journey
    To withered hands.

I thank my Creator for making me
    Daring and whole.
I have come face to face with what is breaking me.
    Once I was beautiful,

The handsomest man in any gathering.
    I enjoyed women who could give.
Even now, I am no mere mumbler of farewells
    Though I have ceased to live.

Bits of that bread you break for me,
    Kindest of my friends,
Fall to the ground among stones and bones
    Or stick in my withered hands.

On a Change in Literary Fashions

A change for the better is to be commended.
   There's one change I
Have decided to follow because it is more
    Profitable for me.

I have ditched my keen poems and their
    Difficult ways
For a common sort of easy art
    That earns me more praise.

My obscure music rankled with
    A picky range
Of people who judged me unworthy of favour.
    Hence the change.

From now on, I renounce the profit of even
    A single penny
If one verse of mine troubles the understanding
    Of anyone in this country.

Free and easy verse on the open road! –
    That's what they want from me.
By the leave of the Earl of Tyrconnell
    That's what they'll get from me.

The dunces of the world would not best me
    At this soft-bellied art.
I have gone out in the rain like the rest –
    A wise man!

I have abandoned – what greater luck? –
    My hard mysterious ways:
I can hear the Earl laughing all night
    At this kind of verse.

Through bad verse many a one is full
    Of love for me this year.
I'd earn even more affection
    But for my fear

Of the Earl, a sharp man who found my
    Hard poems soft to his mind.
It's easy for me to be brave now
    That he is away in England.

Every poem I struggled to compose
    Nearly broke my heart.
This new fashion is the cause of good health
    And bad art.

Henceforth, if anyone finds fault with me,
    His good name is ended.
I have begun to suffer profitably.
    A change for the better is to be commended.

The Shannon

I

Shannon,
How you smile at me
As you still your voice
Westwards towards the sea.

Brooding from Sliabh Iarann
God's fluent work
You speed through Lough Ree
And Lough Derg.

Over Dunass Rapids
You can't be held in check.
Yet you have learned to linger
Gracing west from Limerick.

Strong at our borders
You move
Past all our dwellings
Like a vigorous legend of love.

The Boyne is noble, and the Laune,
And the Suca, but the good books
That are as old as rivers
Say
That you, O Shannon,
Are nobler than they.

II

You flow so truly out of
And into yourself, it would be
Wrong to name you after
Any man of property.

You have a father and a mother.
If sound reasons matter
You flow for all the people,
Every inch of your water

Deepens us.
Fakes and liars and men with a sharp eye
For a profitable prospect would own you.
Flow back into yourself
If you're said by me.

Smooth fish within you,
Smooth men at your side
Cannot make you flow for them alone.
They love only what they can own.
You flow through your own pride.

I will write poems
Attacking those
Who try to own you.
They think in greedy prose.

I have a question,
(May the Christ Who did not own Himself
And yet is all the world
Be blessed forever)

Where is there
A comparable river?

Local despots would grab you
But you belong in all our blood
Like the white blossom on the hazel
In the wood.

Moloney Up and At It
Brendan Kennelly

Moloney Up and At It is a collection of comic poems with a central character, Moloney, who tells of his experiences of, for the most part, sex and death. The language of the poems is that of the south-west of Ireland, of north Kerry in particular. Brendan Kennelly's intention was to capture the easy, bawdy humour, the candid speech and the fluent power of narrative of so many of the men and women he heard telling stories of this kind. Behind these poems is the strong oral tradition of the south, a tradition that still flourishes in certain areas.

The Midnight Court
Brian Merriman
A New Translation by Cosslett Ó Cuinn

This humorous, licentious poem *The Midnight Court*, so full of bawdy, racy language, was written in Irish by the Clare poet, Brian Merriman, in 1780. It has been described as the forerunner of Women's Liberation demanding as it does, the right of all women to sex and marriage and an end to the crusty bachelor moods of the Irish male and the forbidding celibacy of the Irish clergy. The treatment of the theme and the richness of the diction have earned it a large measure of fame, popularity and admiration in the intervening years.

The Midnight Court has been translated into many European languages, and this new translation by Canon Cosslett Quin captures the rich, robust, Rabelaisian humour of the original.

John Verling's magnificent and detailed drawings, which make no attempt to anchor the poem in the eighteenth century, are perfectly suited to its whimsical and permissive mood.